John 3:16

John 3:16

What's It All About?

Murray J. Harris

CASCADE *Books* · Eugene, Oregon

JOHN 3:16
What's It All About?

Copyright © 2015 Murray J. Harris. All rights reserved. Except
for brief quotations in critical publications or reviews, no part of
this book may be reproduced in any manner without prior written permission from the publisher. Write: Permissions. Wipf and
Stock Publishers, 199 W. 8th Ave., Suite 3, Eugene, OR 97401.

Cascade Publications
An Imprint of Wipf and Stock Publishers
199 W. 8th Ave., Suite 3
Eugene, OR 97401

www.wipfandstock.com

ISBN 13: 978-1-4982-2407-9

Cataloguing-in-Publication Data

Harris, Murray J.

John 3:16 : what's it all about? / Murray J. Harris.

xii + 42 p. ; 21 cm. Includes bibliographical references.

ISBN 13: 978-1-4982-2407-9

1. Bible. John III, 16—Criticism, interpretation, etc. I. Title.

BS2615.52 H375 2015

Manufactured in the U.S.A.   05/26/2015

To Oliver and Jane and their spouses,
and to friends far and near

Contents

Acknowledgments

Some material in the text and endnote of this book is drawn from the author's commentary *The Gospel of John* (Nashville, TN: Broadman and Holman, 2015) in the Exegetical Guide to the Greek New Testament (EGGNT) series, and is used with permission.

The translations of ancient documents (including the New Testament) are mine, unless indicated.

I am most grateful to Dr. D. Christopher Spinks, one of the editors at Cascade Books of Wipf and Stock Publishers, for his careful and efficient guidance of this little book through the publication process.

Abbreviations

IN THE ENDNOTES OF this book, customary and well-known abbreviations for reference works, periodicals, biblical and non-biblical references, and English translations have been used. If readers are in any doubt about any abbreviations, they should consult *The SBL Handbook of Style for Ancient Near Eastern, Biblical, and Early Christian Studies,* ed. P. H. Alexander et al. (Peabody, MA: Hendrickson, 1999).

In references to BDAG the letters a, b, c, d denote the four quadrants of the page cited.

Here is the Greek text of John 3:16 as printed by Nestle-Aland (28th ed.) and UBS (4th ed.).

> Οὕτως γὰρ ἠγάπησεν ὁ θεὸς τὸν κόσμον,
> ὥστε τὸν υἱὸν τὸν μονογενῆ ἔδωκεν, ἵνα
> πᾶς ὁ πιστεύων εἰς αὐτὸν μὴ ἀπόληται ἀλλ᾽
> ἔχῃ ζωὴν αἰώνιον

Introduction

SOME MEMORABLE SENTENCES ARE brief and historically poignant, such as "I have a dream" (Martin Luther King), or "Et tu, Brute?" (Julius Caesar, according to William Shakespeare).

Some are longer and amusing, such as Groucho Marx's quip, "I never forget a face, but in your case I'd be glad to make an exception," or Oscar Wilde's wisecrack, "Some cause happiness wherever they go; others, whenever they go."

Still other sentences are proverbial and are associated with key historical figures, such as Winston Churchill's insight, "A pessimist sees the difficulty in every opportunity, an optimist sees the opportunity in every difficulty," or John Fitzgerald Kennedy's challenge, "My fellow Americans, ask not what your country can do for you—ask what you can do for your country."

But perhaps no sentence is more famous than that found in the third chapter and sixteenth verse of the Gospel of John in the New Testament of the Bible (John 3:16). The aim of this work is to examine in detail this crucial sentence that was first written in Greek but now has been translated into hundreds of world languages.

The pattern of this book is simple. In considering the meaning of any sentence, it is necessary to give attention to the wider and the narrower literary *context* of the sentence, for foreign ideas can easily be read into a statement when it is considered out of its context. Then follows an *examination* of each word and phrase in the sentence. This leads into some *final comments* about John 3:16.

The footnotes contain technical material designed for those who have a knowledge of Greek and these footnotes often explain or justify points made in the main text.

The Context of John 3:16

The Fourth Gospel

Matthew, Mark, Luke, and John—these are the first four books of the New Testament section of the Bible. They are called "gospels" because they give an account of the "good news" (the meaning of "gospel") that was brought to the world by Jesus of Nazareth.[1] So "The Gospel of John" is the good news according to John, as understood and recorded by John. His was probably the last of the four Gospels to be written, perhaps during the 80s or 90s of the first century AD. It is sometimes simply called the Fourth Gospel. John had been one of the inner circle of Jesus' disciples called The Twelve.[2] He wrote at the end of a long, rich life, providing accurate recollections of Jesus' life and teaching along with reflections on their significance for his contemporaries.

Like the other three Gospel writers, John probably had two main purposes in writing—to generate and to confirm faith in Jesus as the long-awaited Jewish Messiah and now the Lord of the universe. As he expresses it, "These things have been written that you may believe that Jesus is the Messiah, the Son of God, and that by believing you may experience eternal life in reliance on him" (John 20:31).[3] Secondary aims may have been to provide Jesus' followers with tools for explaining and defending the Christian faith and with details of the words and works of Jesus that would prompt their devotion to him.[4]

When we compare John's Gospel with the other three, we notice that he adds significant material that supplements those earlier Gospels. In fact, about 92 percent of his Gospel is unique to him and only 8 percent is shared with one or more of the others. For example, it is only this Gospel that records a period Jesus spent in Jerusalem and Judea before his main teaching was given in Galilee. And as it happens, the crucial meeting of Jesus and Nicodemus that prompted John 3:16 took place in Jerusalem during that earlier time, perhaps in the year AD 29 just after a celebration of the Jewish festival of Passover.

Introducing Nicodemus

As John sketches the profile of Nicodemus, we learn he was "one of the Pharisees." The term "Pharisee" means "the separated one." Pharisees formed an elite brotherhood of up to 6,000 men whose main concern in life was to observe scrupulously every aspect of the sacred Jewish law as it was set out in the Bible and had been enlarged by lawyers ("scribes") who identified 613 commandments, 248 of them positive in tone ("Do this") and 365 negative in tone ("Don't do this"). At an earlier time the Pharisees had been called the "Hasidim," God's loyal ones. At the time of Jesus they were drawn from all segments of Jewish society and were the living branch of Judaism,[5] as opposed to the Sadducees who were the wealthy aristocracy and were wedded to the status quo.

Another description of Nicodemus that John gives us is that he was "a leading man among the Jews," which indicates he was a member of the Sanhedrin, as John 7:50

explicitly says. The Sanhedrin was the supreme council of the Jews and was sometimes called "the body of elders" or the "senate." The Pharisees were a minority group within the Sanhedrin[6] but among the general populace they had an influence out of all proportion to their numbers.

Later in John's Gospel we discover two other interesting facts about Nicodemus.

He was a champion of due process. The Sanhedrin had tried to arrest Jesus because the populace were inclined to see him as their Messiah who would deliver them from Roman oppression. But Nicodemus pointedly reminded his colleagues that Jewish law gave accused people the right to explain what they were up to—they were "innocent until proven guilty" as we would say. "Is it the way of our law to condemn anyone without first giving him a hearing and finding out what he is about?" (John 7:51).

Also, Nicodemus must have been a very wealthy man. When he and his servants were assisting in the burial of Jesus, he brought with him an enormous quantity of expensive spices—some 35 kilos or 65 pounds—for use in the temporary preservation of Jesus' corpse. Evidently, for Jesus' burial Nicodemus supplied the spices while a certain Joseph of Arimathea provided the grave clothes (John 19:38–40).

This, then, is the Nicodemus who arranged to meet Jesus and discuss his teaching. We are told he approached Jesus "at night." Why was this? Why not talk to Jesus during daylight hours? Perhaps Nicodemus wanted to avoid bad publicity that would come his way if he was seen to be in serious conversation with a wandering teacher who lacked formal training and who hailed from Galilee in the obscure far north—of all places! Also, Jewish rabbis taught that the ideal time to study the law was at night when you are less likely to be disturbed. Nicodemus knew the crowds were flocking around Jesus during the day so that only a night-time visit would allow an uninterrupted conversation away from the crowds.

The Conversation between Nicodemus and Jesus

The conversation falls into two parts. Verses 2–10 form a vigorous dialogue between Nicodemus and Jesus, but at verse 11 the dialogue becomes a monologue on the lips of Jesus that runs down to verse 21.[7] In this monologue, or mini-discourse, Jesus tries to explain in different ways what he had been saying during their conversation. Clearly he believes the observations he has been making throughout are of first-rate importance, for three times (in vv. 3, 5, 11) he prefaces his remarks with a formal phrase that may be literally translated, "Truly, truly, I am telling you." The sense is "I tell you in solemn truth" or "Let me firmly assure you."[8]

In the conversation, Jesus' attention is focussed on Nicodemus, for he uses the (Greek) singular form "you" some five times (vv. 3, 5, 7, 10, 11). But on several occasions he uses the (Greek) plural form "you" (vv. 7, 11 and four times in v. 12) and also speaks of "someone" (vv. 3 and 5) and "everyone" (vv. 8 and 15).[9] This suggests Jesus viewed Nicodemus as a representative of the Jewish nation as a whole and regarded his own teaching about being "born again" as relevant to all people, whether they be Jewish or non-Jewish.

Following Jewish custom, Nicodemus begins the conversation with a compliment. He salutes Jesus as a fellow rabbi although he knew Jesus was relatively young [10] and was not a graduate of any theological school. "Rabbi, we know you have come as a teacher from God. For no one can do these signs that you are doing, unless God is with him."

As was his custom, Jesus chooses not to engage with Nicodemus at a superficial, mundane level and discuss the miraculous signs he had been performing. Rather, he immediately addresses Nicodemus's spiritual condition, the state of his soul. "Jesus gave him this answer, 'I tell you in solemn truth, no one can see the kingdom of God unless he is born again.'" Nicodemus would doubtless have been a little taken aback by the directness of Jesus' reply. He knew that a convert to Judaism was spoken of as being "like a new-born child," but how could the idea of being "born again" apply to someone who was born a Jew? "'How on earth can a man be born once he is old?' countered Nicodemus. 'Surely he cannot re-enter his mother's womb and be born again!'"

Nicodemus has obviously misunderstood Jesus' teaching about new birth, so Jesus explains it further. He is saying, in effect, "Everyone, whether Jew or Gentile, including you, Nicodemus, needs rebirth from above." The term Jesus had used earlier has a double sense: "again" and "from above."[11] The further explanation that Jesus gives is difficult because it is condensed. Here is an expanded paraphrase of what he is saying, instead of a close translation.

> I tell you in solemn truth: No one can enter the kingdom of God unless he or she is reborn as a result of being cleansed from sin by the work of the Spirit of God. What is born by natural birth is a human nature, but what is born by the Spirit's power is a new spiritual nature. You mustn't be surprised that I said to you, "You all must be born again." The wind blows about wherever it wants to. You hear its sound but you cannot tell where it is coming from and where it is going to each time. So, too, is the case with everyone whose birth comes by the Spirit's work—work

that is beyond human control or sight or com-
prehension, but its results are clearly visible.

Nicodemus remains in the dark: "How can this possibly be?" Jesus knew that Nicodemus would have remem-
bered from the Hebrew Scriptures various people who had
experienced a fresh start through God's saving interven-
tion. So he responds with a question of his own. "You are a
distinguished teacher of Israel, yet you do not understand
these things?"

It is at this point that Jesus' dialogue with Nicodemus
becomes a monologue as he tells Nicodemus about his own
role in making spiritual rebirth a possibility for everyone.
Again, an expanded paraphrase will fill out what John has
captured in summary form.

> I tell you in solemn truth: We are talking about
> what we know first-hand and we are testifying to
> what we ourselves have seen; but still you people
> do not accept our testimony. I have been giving
> you teaching concerning spiritual rebirth using
> earthly language about physical birth and the
> wind. If you don't believe that way, how are you
> going to believe if I go on to talk about deeper
> truths such as my role as the Son of Man who
> came down from heaven? In fact, no one has
> ever gone up into heaven except the one who
> first came down from heaven, namely the Son
> of Man. And just as Moses lifted up the serpent
> in the desert so that the Israelites could look up
> and be spared death, so the Son of Man must be
> "lifted up" on the cross and then into heaven,[12]
> so that everyone who believes may have eternal
> life in reliance on him.

This, then, is the wider and narrower context of John
3:16. Our famous sentence is found in the last of the four

Gospels, a record of the deeds and words of Jesus written by John, one of Jesus' closest friends. During a conversation Jesus had with Nicodemus, a leading figure among the Jews of the first century AD, Jesus emphasizes the need for everyone to have a spiritual rebirth that comes about by believing in him.

We are now ready to launch into a detailed examination of our special sentence, in the hope that we will discover exactly what this "believing in Jesus" is all about.

An Examination of John 3:16

"For God so loved the world that he gave his one and only Son, that whoever believes in him shall not perish but have eternal life." (NIV)

For God

THE WORD "FOR," LIKE its Greek equivalent,[13] is a conjunction, a word that joins together two clauses or sentences or sets of ideas.[14] In the present case, "for" links verse 16 with what precedes. It introduces a clarification, explaining how "rebirth from above" (vv. 3–8) became an option for everyone who believes (v. 15). The Greek word often translated "for" has the meaning "you see." This is the way the standard dictionary of New Testament Greek understands the word.[15] "*You see*, God so loved the world. . ."

But exactly who is this "God" (Greek *theos*) who was so in love with the world?

Could it be one of the members of the Triune God, either the Father, or the Son (Jesus Christ) or the Holy Spirit? But nowhere in this Gospel or elsewhere in the New Testament do we read of "God the Holy Spirit." And we cannot identify "God" with "God the Son" because the sentence goes on to tell us that this "God" gave his Son.

This leaves "God the Father" as the only possible referent. And precisely that expression is found in John 6:27: "On this person (Jesus, the Son of Man[16]) *God the Father* has put his seal of approval." When we examine the eighty-three uses of the word "God" (*theos*) in the Fourth Gospel, we discover that in many contexts "the Father" is an alternative way of referring to God. Consider these examples.

> John 6:45–46 "It is written in the Prophets: 'And they will all be taught by God.' Everyone who has listened to the Father and has learned from him comes to me. Not that anyone has seen the Father—only the one who is from God has seen the Father."

> John 13:3 "Jesus knew that the Father had committed everything into his hands, and that he had come from God and was returning to God."

> John 20:17 "Jesus told her, 'Don't cling to me, for I have not yet ascended to the Father. Instead, go to my brothers and tell them, "I am ascending to my Father and your Father, to my God and your God."'"

Moreover, in the common expression, "Son of God" (nine examples in the Fourth Gospel) God must be the Father. In fact, there are only four places among the eighty-three instances of the term *theos* where "God" could *not* refer to the Father.[17]

Only one conclusion is possible. In John 3:16 "God" refers to God the Father.

so loved

If we fill out the meaning of "so," we find there are basically two options.

1. "In this way" or "as follows."[18]

Several English versions adopt this option:

> "For God loved the world in this way: He gave His One and Only Son" (Holman Christian Study Bible)

> "For this is how God loved the world: he gave his only Son" (New Jerusalem Bible; similarly International Standard Version; New English Translation Bible)

This is a perfectly possible translation. The only question is whether this translation does justice to the rest of the sentence. "God loved . . . in this way" comes across as a decidedly flat and almost clinical way of introducing a mind-boggling statement: wonder of wonders, God actually sent into the world and gave over to death his most treasured possession—his one and only Son!

2. "To such an extent" or "so much" or "so intensely."[19]

This rendering fits nicely with the stupendous assertion that follows.

> "For so greatly did God love the world that He gave His only Son" (Weymouth; similarly Moffatt, "so dearly").

> "God loved the world so much that he gave his only Son" (NEB; similarly Contemporary English Version; Goodspeed; New Living Translation)

Another reason for preferring this sense of "so" is the unusual position of the word "loved" in Greek which makes it particularly emphatic: this was no ordinary love![20] "God loved the world to such an extraordinary extent that he gave . . ."

There are two Greek verbs used in John's Gospel that may be translated "love." Some see a difference between them, claiming that *phileō* refers to a passionate, more intimate affection, while *agapaō* describes a more elevated, reasoned love. But such a distinction is not supported by the evidence. The two verbs are usually interchangeable, as when we read that the Father loves the Son in 3:35 (using *agapaō*) and in 5:20 (using *phileō*).[21] So when Jesus says in John 3:16 that God *loved* the world (using *agapaō*) the love being spoken of is not a carefully reasoned love as opposed to a passionate love. From the immediate context it is clearly a strong, selfless, gift-giving love that is totally focussed on the welfare of others. The gift being given as an expression of love is phenomenal, beyond all expectation and unrelated to any particular merit in the recipients.

In our sentence the past tense of "loved" matches the past tense of "gave." God loved and gave. His gift expressed his love. It is not that God had all along disliked the human race and then suddenly decided that he really ought to love them and give them a gift to prove that. No, his warm love for his creatures had always been there, but at one point in time he expressed it in an unparalleled love-gift.[22]

Nor does the past tense of "loved" imply that at the present time God no longer cares about humans. While there is no comparable statement in John's Gospel that says that God loves all humans, the open-ended and timeless guarantee that "everyone who believes" will gain eternal life (John 3:16) proves the Father's ongoing love for all.[23]

the world

A glance at the Oxford English Dictionary or Webster's American Dictionary of the English Language will show how varied is the use of the word "world" in modern speech and writing. Think, for example, of the following phrases, many of them colloquial, illustrating that range. How goes the world with you? What will the world say? Are you up with the scientific world? That will do him a world of good! This is the best of all possible worlds. She means the world to me. All the world's a stage. That prize-winning novelist is world famous.[24]

So it comes as no surprise that the Greek word for world—*kosmos*—has a similarly wide range of meanings, even in the Fourth Gospel.

Sometimes it refers to *planet earth*. "Anyone who walks in daylight does so without stumbling, for he sees by this world's light [= the sun]" (John 11:9).

Sometimes *kosmos* means *the place where humans live*. "A woman giving birth to a child has pain because her time has come; but once her baby is born she forgets her suffering because of her joy that a human being has been born into the world" (John 16:21).

Sometimes it denotes *the whole universe*, the sum total of everything. "So now, Father, glorify me in your presence with the glory I had with you before the world existed" (John 17:5).

What is especially interesting is that in the sentence that follows 3:16 *kosmos* occurs three times. "For God did not send his Son into the *world* to condemn the *world*, but to save the *world* through him" (3:17). In the first case, "the world" is the earth in contrast to heaven; in the second, it means humans in general; in the third, all humans without distinction or exception.

But there is one meaning of "world" that is found in John's Gospel but not in any English dictionary. Often in this Gospel there are ominous, negative ideas attaching to the term *kosmos*. The world is evil and needs a savior. So the inhabitants of a small town in Samaria called Jesus "the Savior of the world" (John 4:42). Consider the following examples of this negative sense.

> John 1:10 "He [Jesus the Logos] was in the world, and the world was made by him, yet the *world* did not recognize him."

> John 7:7 "The *world* . . . hates me because I bring evidence against it that what it does is evil."

> John 16:8, 11 "When he [the Holy Spirit] comes, he will convict the *world* of guilt in regard to sin and righteousness and judgment . . . ; in regard to judgment, because the prince of this *world* [= the devil] now stands condemned."

> John 16:33 "I have told you these things so that you may find your peace in me. In this *world* you will have suffering. But take courage! I have conquered the *world.*"

So what does all this mean for "the world" in John 3:16? There it refers to "all humans without distinction or exception" (= the third sense in 3:17) in spite of the fact that we are part of a world that is hostile to God and alienated from him. This makes the love of God all the more unprecedented and astonishing. God's love knows no bounds in its intensity (it is limitless) or in its scope (it includes all humans).

that he gave

Here are two sentences.

> He ran as fast as he could *that* he might win the race.

> He ran so quickly *that* he won the race.

If we were writing these two sentences in Greek, the word for "that" could be *hōste*. In the first case "that" introduces a purpose; in the second case it introduces a result. Now for a fascinating fact—although it is technical! While there are a few examples in the New Testament where *hōste* introduces a purpose and many places where it introduces a result, there are only two very special places where the result is expressed by what is called the "indicative mood"—and one is John 3:16![25]

The other example of this construction is found in Paul's letter to the Galatian Christians where he is speaking about Peter's unfortunate decision in a city called Antioch to avoid contact with those Christians who happened to be non-Jews. He then comments, "Along with him [Peter] the rest of the [Christian] Jews there played the hypocrite, with the result that even Barnabas was led astray by their hypocrisy" (Gal 2:13). Barnabas was one of Paul's closest friends and his "play-acting" was a great surprise and disappointment to Paul. Another English translation puts it this way: "And the rest of the Jews put on the same act as he [Peter] did, so that even Barnabas was carried away by their insincerity."[26]

What light does all this throw on John 3:16? It shows that the grammatical construction used in our sentence places all the emphasis on the actual result of God's loving the world so immeasurably. The focus is on the effect rather than the cause.[27] The sense is, "If you can believe it, God did not spare his one and only Son but actually surrendered him for the benefit of his rebellious creatures."[28] This is not some abstract affection for his creatures, but love-in-action—and sacrificial action at that.

We know what God's gift was—his one and only Son (see the next section). But what was involved in the act of giving itself? Again, the context is crucial, both what precedes and what follows.

Immediately after 3:16 we read that "God sent his Son into the world." So one aspect of the "giving" was the Father's despatching of his Son on a mission to "the place where humans live" (= the first meaning of "the world" in 3:17).[29] John has already spoken of this in John 1:14: "the Word became flesh,"[30] that is, Jesus Christ as the Son of God was the full expression ("the Word") of God the Father and became a fully human person, taking on a complete and genuine human existence. Theologians call this the "incarnation."

But an earlier sentence adds another dimension to the giving. In 3:14 mention is made of a painful (literally!) episode in the history of the nation of Israel. After their deliverance from Egypt in the famous Exodus, the Israelites wandered about in the Sinai Peninsula for many long years on their way to the Promised Land. During that time the people impatiently grumbled against God and Moses. When God sent poisonous snakes to punish his rebellious people, Moses interceded with God on their behalf and was told to make a bronze snake and erect it on a pole and that anyone bitten by a snake who looked at the elevated bronze snake would live.[31] Jesus reminds Nicodemus of this story with the comment, "Just as Moses lifted up the snake in the desert, so the Son of Man must be lifted up." We have already seen here a play on words by which "lifted up" refers to the crucifixion when Jesus would be "lifted up" on to a

Roman cross to die, as well as referring to his being "lifted up" to heaven by his resurrection from the dead. By that death on the cross he would "take away the sin of the world" (John 1:29) as John the Baptist had boldly announced a short while earlier.

We conclude, then, that God's "giving" of his Son involved two things—God sent him into the world as a person who was completely human and then surrendered him to a death that would solve the world's sin problem. In a very similar passage elsewhere, John says, "God sent his Son to be the atoning sacrifice for our sins" (1 John 4:10).[32] In a nutshell, God's giving involved the incarnation and crucifixion of Jesus.[33] No wonder another New Testament author says, "Thank God for his gift that is indescribable!" (Paul in 2 Cor 9:15). Human words are inadequate to express the magnificence of Jesus Christ and the salvation he brings.

his one and only Son

Thus far we have considered what God's act of giving entailed. Now our focus needs to be on the actual gift given—a special Son, no less.[34]

As God's Son, Jesus possessed his Father's nature. There can be no doubt that John's Gospel portrays Jesus as fully divine. When Jesus called God "his own Father," his Jewish opponents recognized that he was "making himself equal with God" (John 5:18). The climax came when he asserted, "I and the Father are one" (John 10:30). He was saying, "My Father and I share the same nature while remaining distinct persons." Little wonder that some of them there and then picked up stones with the intent of stoning him to death. Jesus, however, continued to dialogue with them.

And toward the end of this Gospel, we learn that one of Jesus' followers, at first a thoroughgoing sceptic about Jesus' resurrection, feels compelled to address Jesus with the telling words, "My Lord and my God!" (John 20:28). Thomas had come to realize that as "Lord" Jesus shared his Father's authority over all creation and all humanity, and as "God" Jesus was one with his Father in nature.

As God's Son, Jesus was uniquely qualified to reveal his Father's character, to tell us exactly and accurately what God is like. Imagine, for a moment, that you are at someone's funeral. First one person, then another, speaks in glowing terms about the deceased. But their tributes sound somewhat unreal and remote, as if they had only a superficial knowledge of the dead man. Finally, the man's spouse speaks from her heart, and you think, "This is for real. Here is someone who has known our friend all his life and in all types of circumstances. Her tribute rings true because it is spoken out of the experience of a lifetime."

Why is Jesus supremely well qualified to describe God for us? It is because as the Son of God he had always been in his Father's presence, in intimate and loving dialogue with him, sharing all his secrets, embracing all his plans. John 1:18 puts it this way. "No one has ever seen God, but the only Son, who is God by nature and at his Father's side, has made him known." Jesus Christ has made the invisible nature of God visible to us all.

The phrase "one and only" is a fine way of translating a single colorful Greek word. *Monogenēs* refers to the only child in a family, someone who is without siblings, someone who is "of sole descent."[35] So then, in God's spiritual family Jesus is without siblings and without equals. No one else can lay claim to the title Son of God in the sense in which it applies to Jesus.[36] He is "unique"—which is another possible meaning of *monogenēs*.[37] Like nobody else had ever done or could do, Jesus exposed his Father's heart of love for all to see. He is the supreme revealer of God as he really is.

Of course, in a human family any child who is without brothers or sisters is especially loved. So, too, in the case of Jesus. His Father loved him dearly,[38] so giving him to a rebellious world and surrendering him to a horrible death was all the harder and is all the more amazing.

Two points emerge. First, the content of God's gift was beyond imagination: this gift was not some earthly monarch or angelic ambassador, but his one and only *Son*. Second, the value of God's gift was beyond calculation: this gift was not some person that could be easily duplicated or replaced, but his *one and only* Son.

that whoever believes in him

Thus far the focus of the sentence has been on the size and uniqueness of God's love-gift. Never before had there been a gift of this magnitude, nor would there ever be another like it.

But what was the purpose and outcome of this magnificent act of giving? Did God simply want to dazzle people with his generosity? Or was there a more noble purpose? Indeed there was.

Here we come across another "that." Earlier, in the phrase "*that* he gave," this word introduced a result. This time "that" translates a different Greek conjunction, *hina*, that normally expresses a purpose ("in order that") but sometimes a result ("so that"). Here it probably introduces both purpose *and* result. Unfortunately our English language cannot catch both senses at the same time, but Greek can. English speakers are locked into choosing between "that whoever believes in him *should* not perish" (= purpose) and "that whoever believes in him *shall* not perish" (result). But we must not forget that, in any case, a result is an achieved purpose!

Those Jews who heard Jesus speak these words would already have been taken aback to hear that God loved all the people of "the world." Their literature had restricted God's special love to the nation of Israel: "his love toward Israel endures forever" (Ezra 3:11). But now Jesus is going even further and giving an open and warm invitation to all and sundry—"whoever believes" or "everyone who believes."[39] This means no one is excluded from the invitation for any reason. Traditional barriers of race or class have been removed; the playing field is perfectly flat, so to speak.

"Whoever believes in him." The "him" is clearly the Son whom God gave, namely Jesus himself. But those who believe in Jesus are not believing in a crucified and buried Jewish prophet. He is a person who snapped the chains of death and now lives for ever in his Father's presence, sharing God's throne.[40]

For good reason John's Gospel has sometimes been called "the Gospel of Belief," for the verb "believe" (*pisteuō*) is used some ninety-eight times.

Sometimes it is *facts* that are believed. In these cases "believe" means "be convinced that" or "believe that."

> John 9:18 "The Jews refused to *believe that* he (the man born blind) had in fact been blind and had gained his sight until they sent for the man's parents."

> John 16:27 "The Father himself loves you because you have loved me and have *become convinced that* I came from God."

> John 20:31 "These signs have been recorded so that you may *believe that* Jesus is the Messiah, the Son of God."

Other times it is *words* that are believed, as when we read that a certain royal official "*believed the word* Jesus had spoken to him and went on his way" (John 4:50).

But when *persons* are believed, John uses two different constructions. In the first construction the verb *pisteuō* is followed by the Greek dative case, and means "believe someone's testimony."

> John 4:21 "Jesus declared, '*Believe what I say*, good woman, a time is coming when you will worship the Father neither on this mountain nor in Jerusalem.'"

The second construction is John's own distinctive idiom. *Pisteuō* is followed by a small word (the preposition *eis*) that indicates the direction of the belief, the object of faith, if you will. To believe *in* Jesus is to have faith that is directed towards him, faith that is focussed on him. All but nine of the forty-five New Testament uses of this construction are found in the Fourth Gospel or John's First Epistle.[41]

It is not merely that we are being asked to believe certain facts about Jesus or believe that all his teaching is true. The belief that is being spoken about, and that is reflected in John's new idiom, is all-encompassing. It involves the total commitment of one's whole self to the person of Christ as Messiah and Lord for ever. This is anything but an easy "believe-ism"! Other parts of John's Gospel describe believing in Jesus as coming to him, as receiving him, as drinking the spiritual water he offers, as following him, and as loving him.[42] When we believe in Jesus we are entrusting ourselves to him forever, relying on him for our acceptance by God and devoting ourselves to serving him.

This "believing" is no short-term feeling, an impression that stays for a while but then fades away as quickly as it came. An open-ended commitment is involved, a permanent all-of-life experience.[43]

So, then, there is a "believing *that*" and a "believing *in*." Perhaps a chart will highlight the differences.

Believing that	Believing in
Deals with facts	Deals with a person
Involves the mind	Involves the heart
Involves recognition of the truth	Involves allegiance to Jesus, the Truth
Can be momentary	Must be continuous
Alters nothing	Alters everything
Is a natural experience	Is a "rebirth from above"
Is a prerequisite	Is the proper outcome

The other most important New Testament writer—Paul—uses a startling metaphor to describe what believing in Jesus means or how a "believer" is related to the risen Jesus. He calls himself a "slave of Christ Jesus" (Rom 1:1)! A slave, someone who belongs "lock, stock, and barrel" to the Supreme Master who is also the Lord of the Universe. So to believe in Jesus, to be his slave, is the highest privilege there is.

shall not perish

We have seen that this phrase expresses a result (as well as a purpose): "that whoever believes in him shall not perish."

We talk about *perishing* cold that makes work or concentration difficult. Or if we strongly reject some idea, we might say, "*Perish* the thought!" When power goes off, food in the fridge or freezer can be ruined or *perish*. But only this last sense of "perish" begins to come close to its meaning in 3:16.

Again the context comes to our aid. Our sentence ends with the words, "shall not perish but have eternal life." Clearly "perishing" and "having eternal life" are opposites, so "perish" will mean "suffer eternal death,"[44] that is, be permanently separated from God, the only source of true life. This may be why some English translations render the phrase, "so that everyone who believes in him may not be lost."[45] To be forever exiled from God is indeed to "be lost."

A further clue to the meaning of "perish" comes from the next sentence that also mentions opposites. "For God did not send his Son into the world to condemn the world, but to save the world through him (Jesus)." To "perish" is to be condemned in God's court, to have his justified anger resting on one's head. As John put it later, "Whoever believes in the Son has eternal life, but whoever refuses to believe in the Son will not see life; instead, God's wrath remains on them" (John 3:36). A chilling prospect, if there ever was one.

All this means God is engaged in a massive rescue operation. In his conversation with Nicodemus, Jesus had already referred to an earlier rescue mission when God told Moses to construct a bronze snake and put it on a pole so that anyone suffering from a poisonous snake bite could look up at the elevated snake and be healed, and so escape death.

In this second and far greater rescue mission, God makes a promise to all those who believe in his Son. He promises to deliver them from perishing—that is, from eternal death, from being lost, and from final condemnation in his court. And the "not" in "shall not perish" means "not ever" or "never." Later Jesus made this even clearer when he said, "I tell you in solemn truth, if anyone keeps my word, they will *never ever* see death" (John 8:51) where Jesus is promising not exemption from physical death but the avoidance of eternal death. Or again, "I give them eternal life, and they will *never ever* perish; no one can tear them from my grasp" (John 10:28).[46]

But why was a rescue operation needed at all? Why was God not satisfied with the status quo? The answer is simply that the natural state of humans is one of lostness, being alienated from a holy God because of our evil ways; God is eager to restore us to a right relationship with himself.

But the major part of God's salvage campaign is positive—a rescue *for* to match the rescue *from*. We now turn to the final part of our sentence to learn about this positive benefit of believing.

but have eternal life

"But" introduces the second and more important result of believing. The first and negative result was this: believers shall not perish. The second and positive result, and the main point, is this: they will have eternal life.[47] It is simply for the sake of English style that most translations omit a "shall" or "will" before "have." In any case, that "shall" or "will" simply refers to any time after the "believing," not to some distant future.

Also, this conjunction ("but") forms a bridge between the two alternatives: ". . . shall not perish *but instead* have eternal life."[48] These two alternatives are mutually exclusive and there is no third alternative. If we choose not to believe, we will perish; if we choose to believe, we will have eternal life. The following sentences (vv. 17–21) spell out these two alternatives.

- being condemned as a non-believer vs. being saved as a believer

- loving darkness and hating the light vs. living by the truth and coming into the light

Now consider the word "have" in the following sentences.

> I *have* a dog called Rover.

> Do you *have* something to eat?

> Everyone who pays their fees will *have* unlimited access to the gym.

In the first case, "have" stands for "own." In the second, "have" means "have available." In the third, "have" = "get and enjoy" or "obtain and have the privilege of."

It is this third use of "have" that is relevant for the phrase "have eternal life." That is, "Everyone who believes . . . will obtain and enjoy the possession of eternal life."[49] The acquisition lies in the future only in the sense it is dependent on believing. But once there is belief, eternal life is a present reality. So then, the "having" is both getting and possessing. Let us remember, however, that this "getting" is not because we deserve eternal life or have done anything to merit it. It comes as a gift. "God gave . . . so that whoever believes in Jesus shall . . . have eternal life."

This leads us to a final and crucial question. What did Jesus and John mean by "eternal life"? Is it simply "living for ever" or does it refer, first of all, to a quality of life?

Let's begin by considering the two words separately. "Life" translates the word *zōē*—yes, the girl's name Zoe! In John's Gospel *zōē* never means "existence" in an abstract sense, nor does it refer to natural, physical life or to the biological existence that humans share with animals.[50] It is the supernatural divine life that God and Christ have by nature and that God gives to humans under certain conditions. So John observes that Jesus himself is life (John 11:25; 14:6) and came to bring life to others (John 10:10).

The Greek behind "eternal" is *aiōnios*, a word that originally meant "belonging to the Age to Come." But because that future Age is unending, this adjective came to mean "eternal." As applied to God, it has the meaning "without beginning or end"[51]—what a mind-boggling reality! In reference to past time, it means "long ago." But applied to anything else, its sense is "with a beginning but without end," that is, "of unending duration" or "destined to last forever."[52]

So when we put the two words together—"eternal life"—they refer to supernatural divine life that lasts forever. Our author, John, uses the phrase "eternal life" seventeen times in his Gospel[53] and, very conveniently, provides us with an illuminating definition of the phrase in the course of recording a prayer in which Jesus addresses his Father, "This is what eternal life is: that they (believers) may know you, the only true God, and know Jesus Christ, whom you have sent" (John 17:3).[54] To "know" God is to have intimate fellowship with him, and this comes by knowing Jesus Christ who revealed his Father.

Clearly, then, "eternal life" is both present and future. It involves "knowing" Jesus and God here and now, but this knowledge will continue for ever. These two tenses of eternal life are expressed elsewhere in this Gospel.

> John 5:24 "I tell you in solemn truth, whoever hears my word and believes him who sent me *has eternal life* and will not be condemned. In fact, they have crossed over from death into life"

> John 11:25–26 "Jesus said to her (Martha) 'I am the resurrection and the (eternal) life. The

person who believes in me *will live*, even though they die. And whoever is alive (spiritually) and believes in me *will never die*"[55]

To summarize. In the phrase "eternal life,"

- "life" (*zōē* in Greek) refers to *quality*: it is a supernatural, spiritual life that comes from God and enables us to share his life.

- "eternal" (*aiōnios* in Greek) refers to *quantity*: this "life" will continue forever.[56] And in this phrase the emphasis certainly rests on "life" rather than on "eternal."[57]

This is where our earlier discussion of the context of John 3:16 becomes relevant. Getting eternal life is the same as being "reborn from above." And just as rebirth implies change, so too does obtaining eternal life. That change happens when we believe in Jesus Christ, when we entrust ourselves to him forever, "lock, stock, and barrel."

Let me end this grammatical analysis of John 3:16 by offering an expanded paraphrase of the sentence that incorporates many of the observations we have made.

> *This rebirth from above is possible for everyone who believes, because God the Father loved all humans to such an extraordinary extent that he actually sent his dearly loved one and only Son into the world and then gave him over to an atoning death, so that everyone, without distinction or exception, who believes in Jesus will not suffer God's wrath and thus be lost, but, on the contrary, will both now and in the hereafter enjoy intimate fellowship with God and actually share in God's own life.*

Final Comments

OF COURSE, JOHN 3:16 is not the *totality* of the gospel ("the good news") nor a summary of the entire New Testament. How could one sentence of twenty-five words (in Greek) possibly sum up the message of nine different authors writing over some forty years?[58] But this sentence *is* a summary of the message of the Fourth Gospel and it does sum up the *essence* of the "good news" which is the *invitation* given to all to believe in Jesus, God's Son, and the *promise* that those who do this will avoid God's condemnation and will share in the very life of God forever.

Now, understandably, someone may say, "Who wants 'eternal life' anyway? It sounds like a boring and endlessly long weekend at the beach when it's raining." In response, let me use six adjectives to sketch what the New Testament as a whole says about the life to come for believers in Jesus.[59]

1. *Embodied*

Christians do not long to be free of the body. Rather, they eagerly wait for a new body like Jesus' resurrection body that God has promised. Paul described it as being

- "spiritual," in the sense of being revitalized and guided by God's Spirit
- "imperishable," free from decay and death

- "glorious," having radiant and unsurpassed beauty

- "powerful," with limitless energy and perfect health

- "heavenly," perfectly adapted to the ecology of heaven

2. *Localized*

Although heaven is a condition, that of knowing and serving God, it is also a place, the locality where God's presence is perfectly expressed and felt. Peter speaks of "a new heaven and a new earth in which righteousness will have its permanent home." Both time and space will no longer be limiting factors.

3. *Personal*

When the physical body of the Christian believer is transformed into a spiritual body like Christ's, their personal identity will be preserved. They are not absorbed into some supreme Being. No, from first to last God treats us as distinctive individuals.

4. *Active*

There will be relief from toil, and yet happy activity that is without exertion or frustration. Believers will joyfully and enthusiastically "follow the Lamb (Jesus) wherever he goes" and share Jesus' reign over the new universe.

5. *Corporate*

Heaven will not be millions of individuals living in personal fellowship with God but in isolation from other worshippers. The City of God will be the capital of the new universe whose inhabitants will live together in a perfect society.

6. *Permanent*

Believers' individual and corporate life with God will be unending. After believers have been raised from the dead, they will be deathless and will experience a perennial rejuvenation that will equip them for the enjoyment and service of God "forever and ever." Also unending will be the excitement of discovering more and more of the inexhaustible nature of God.

John 3:16 presents us all with an invitation and a promise that call for a response.

Notes

1. Our English word "gospel" comes from the Old English word, *gōdspel* (*gōd*, "good," and *spel*, "news") referring to the "glad tidings" preached by Christ and, more generally, the whole revelation brought by Christ. Then the term was applied to the record of Christ's life and teaching found in Matthew, Mark, Luke, and John; thus, "The gospel according to Matthew/Mark/Luke/John." Finally these four records themselves were called the Gospels. There is only one gospel, but there are four Gospels.

2. Until the early nineteenth century, church tradition almost unanimously maintained that the author of the Fourth Gospel was the apostle John, the son of Zebedee (Mark 1:19–20; 10:35) and brother of James (Acts 12:2). But many modern scholars argue that the internal evidence provided by the Gospel itself points to another person (such as John the Elder [2 John 1] or the "Beloved Disciple" [John 13:23]) or group (such as the leaders of a "Johannine community") as the author(s). For a discussion of all the relevant issues, see Craig S. Keener, *The Gospel of John. A Commentary* (Peabody, MA: Hendrickson, 2003) 1:81–115. I shall be assuming that the author is the Apostle John and that he is to be identified with "the disciple whom Jesus loved" (the Beloved Disciple).

3. Although three important proto-Alexandrian MSS (p⁶⁶ᵛⁱᵈ ℵ* B) read ἵνα πιστεύητε (*hina pisteuēte*, present subjunctive), representatives of the later Alexandrian text-type (C L W 33 1241) along with Western (D) and Byzantine (A N Δ 700 1010 1424 *Byz Lect*) witnesses read ἵνα πιστεύσητε (*hina pisteusēte*, aorist subjunctive). The UBS⁴ Committee "had difficulty in deciding which variant to place in the text" (B. M. Metzger, *A Textual Commentary on the Greek New*

Testament, 2nd ed. [Stuttgart: German Bible Society, 1994] 14*, 219–20). It is often claimed that the difference between the two tenses may be expressed by "that you may continue to believe" (present, NRSV footnote; cf. NEB text, "that you may hold the faith") and "that you may come to believe" (aorist, NRSV; NEB footnote). That *could* be the difference between the two readings, but we should not overlook two facts: (1) John uses the present tense of πιστεύω (*pisteuō*) to denote both coming to faith and continuing in faith (e.g., John 6:29). (2) The aorist tense simply states a bald fact ("that you may believe") without in itself specifying the nature of the action involved, whether it be progressive, iterative, or punctiliar. The preferred reading is ἵνα πιστεύσητε and may point to either ongoing or single action, that is, it may refer to continuing to believe or coming to faith. (The idea of repeated action is inappropriate with the verb πιστεύω). This means that neither a pastoral nor an evangelistic aim should be excluded on the basis of 20:31 alone; the intended audience may well be both Christians and non-Christians.

4. Each of the four Evangelists probably had the four aims mentioned (P–E–A–L) among other purposes:

Pastoral: to enrich the faith of Christians by giving instruction regarding Christian teaching.

Evangelistic: to generate faith in Jesus as Messiah and Lord among non-believers.

Apologetic: to justify faith in the case of both believers and potential believers.

Liturgical: to provide documents suitable for public reading to promote worship.

5. On the Pharisees, see S. Westerholm, "Pharisees," in *Dictionary of Jesus and the Gospels,* ed. J. B. Green, S. McKnight, and I. H. Marshall (Downers Grove, IL: InterVarsity, 1992) 609–14.

6. The Sanhedrin comprised three groups:

οἱ ἀρχιερεῖς (*hoi archiereis*), "the high priests," the current high priest, all ex-high priests, and some family members (cf. Acts 4:6); most of these were Sadducees;

οἱ πρεσβύτεροι (*hoi presbyteroi*), "elders," the lay nobility; and

οἱ Φαρισαῖοι (*hoi Pharisaioi*), "Pharisees," including the scribes/lawyers.

7. There is uncertainty where the words of Jesus end. Some English versions place quotation marks after v. 15 (TCNT, Weymouth, Goodspeed, RSV, Barclay, NAB[2], Cassirer, TNIV, ESV) but most more recent translations end Jesus' words after v. 21 (NASB[1, 2], NAB[1], NEB, REB, JB, NJB, NIV[1, 2], NRSV, NLT, HCSB). In favor of the latter option: γάρ (*gar*) more naturally establishes a link with vv. 14–15 than introduces John's theological reflection; the two phrases πᾶς ὁ πιστεύων (*pas ho pisteuōn*) and ἔχῃ ζωὴν αἰώνιον (*echē zōēn aiōnion*) in v. 16b appear to be intentionally resumptive of the same phrases in v. 15; the phrase ὁ θεὸς . . . τὸν υἱὸν . . . ἔδωκεν (*ho theos . . . ton huion . . . edōken*) probably alludes to the death by crucifixion referred to in 14b; there is no indication of a transition from Jesus' words to John's reflection; there seems to be a trinitarian inclusiveness in Jesus' words about divine agency in regeneration, from the Spirit (vv. 5–8) to the Son of Man (vv. 13–15) to God the Father (vv. 16–21) (on this last point see R. E. Brown, *The Gospel According to John (i-xii)* [Garden City, NY: Doubleday, 1966] 136, citing the work of F. Roustang). It is no difficulty for this view that Jesus speaks of himself in vv. 16–19 in the third person; he had already done so in vv. 13–14 ("Son of Man"). But even if vv. 16–21 are in fact John's reflections on the preceding words of Jesus, as some commentators hold, the sentence of 3:16 is equally authoritative, for there is no difference between the voice of the earthly Jesus and the voice of the risen Jesus communicated to John through his Spirit.

8. Ἀμὴν ἀμὴν λέγω σοι (*Amēn amēn legō soi*) (vv. 3, 5, 11). Ἀμήν, the Greek transliteration of the Hebrew ʾāmēn ("surely," "let it be so") denotes a "strong affirmation of what is stated" (BDAG 53c). Whereas this solemn attestation is always single in the three Synoptic Gospels (e.g., ἀμὴν λέγω ὑμῖν, *amēn legō hymin*, Matt 6:2) in the Fourth Gospel it is always double, twenty times with λέγω ὑμῖν and five times with λέγω σοι.

9. Singular: σοι (*soi*) vv. 3, 5, 7, 11; συ (*sy*), v. 10; plural: ὑμᾶς (*hymas*), v. 7; ὑμῖν (*hymin*) (v. 12 twice); λαμβάνετε (*lambanete*), v. 11; πιστεύετε . . . πιστεύσετε (*pisteuete . . . pisteusete*) v. 12. Τις (*tis*) vv. 3, 5; πᾶς (*pas*), vv. 8, 15.

10. Jesus was probably in his early thirties, since he was born before the death of Herod the Great (Matt 2:1), which occurred in 4 BC. See H. W. Hoehner, "Chronology," in *Dictionary of Jesus and the Gospels* (Downers Grove, IL: InterVarsity, 1992) 118–22.

11. There is clearly a word play intended, since ἄνωθεν (*anōthen*) (vv. 3, 7) can mean both "again/anew" and "from above" (BDAG 92 b–d); "rebirth from above" (= by God) catches both senses.

12. As with ἄνωθεν (see previous footnote) there is an intentional double meaning. The verb ὑψόω (*hypsoō*) ("lift up") refers to Jesus' being lifted up on to his cross and to his being lifted up (= exalted) to heaven through his resurrection/ascension; "the heavenly exaltation presupposes the earthly [John] 8:28; 12:32" (BDAG 1046a).

13. Γάρ (*Gar*) is sometimes causal or inferential but its most common use is explanatory, although in narrative it may simply mark a transition (see BDAG 189a–190a).

14. Those who argue that Jesus' words end at v. 15 point out that γάρ (*gar*) sometimes marks a transition to John's theological reflections (e.g., 6:64; 7:39) or asides (e.g., 4:9; 20:9).

15. BDAG 189d.

16. The title "Son of Man" was Jesus' favorite self-designation and derived its meaning primarily from Dan 7:13–14 where somebody "like a son of man" is a divine figure to whom the Ancient of Days gives sovereign power and a kingdom, and from Isa 52:13 that speaks of God's obedient Servant who "will be raised and lifted up and highly exalted."

17. These places are 1:1 (θεὸς ἦν ὁ λόγος, *theos ēn ho logos*, of the preexistent Logos); 1:18 (μονογενὴς θεός, *monogenēs theos*, of the Only Son); 10:34–35 (θεοί . . . θεούς, *theoi . . . theous*, of unscrupulous human judges); and 20:28 (ὁ θεός μου, *ho theos mou*, addressed to Jesus). At least three facts make it highly improbable that John intends any distinction to be drawn between ὁ θεός and θεός, as if between the Father and the Son or the Son and the Father: (1) In prepositional phrases θεός occurs 22 times, 12 times with the article and 10 times without. (2) When it is used with the prepositions παρά (*para*) (+ genitive) and ἐκ (*ek*), θεός sometimes has the article (παρά: 5:44; 6:46; 8:40; 16:27 *v.l.*; ἐκ: 7:17; 8:42, 47 twice) and sometimes lacks it (παρά: 1:6; 9:16, 33; ἐκ: 1:13). (3) In 19:7 John has υἱὸς θεοῦ (*huios theou*) but writes ὁ υἱὸς τοῦ θεοῦ in 1:34, 49; 3:18; 5:25; 10:36 (υἱὸς τοῦ θεοῦ); 11:4, 27; 20:31. Similarly, compare τέκνα θεοῦ (*tekna theou*) in 1:12 with τὰ τέκνα τοῦ θεοῦ (*ta tekna tou theou*) in 11:52. The canon of Apollonius and "Colwell's Rule" may apply in some of these examples.

18. BDAG (742b under #2) lists John 3:16 under the heading "pert[aining] to what follows in discourse material, *in this way, as follows*," but in the preceding parallel cited (SIG 1169, 57–58) οὕτω . . . ὥστε (*houtō . . . hōste*) is rendered "to such an extent . . . that" (see n. 19 below).

19. LSJ 1277 s.v. οὕτως (*houtōs*) III.1, "*to such an extent, so, so much, so very, so excessively*," noting that οὕτως is frequently followed by ὡς (*hōs*) or ὥστε (*hōste*) (citing Herodotus 1.32 and Xenophon, *Anabasis*, 7.4.3). BDAG (742b under #3) describes οὕτω/οὕτως as a "marker of a relatively high degree, *so*, before adj. and adv. . . . Before a verb *so intensely*" (citing Xenophon, *Cyropaedia*, 1.3.11; *Testament of Abraham*, B 4 p. 108, line 11; Tatian 19.1; and 1 John 4:11 ['Αγαπητοί, εἰ οὕτως ὁ θεὸς ἠγάπησεν ἡμᾶς, . . . , *Agapētoi, ei houtōs ho theos ēgapēsen hēmas*, . . .]). This latter passage is verbally close to John 3:16.

20. Οὕτως γὰρ ἠγάπησεν ὁ θεὸς τὸν κόσμον (*houtōs gar ēgapēsen ho theos ton kosmon*).

21. Other examples of the interchangeability of these two verbs: Jesus is said to love Lazarus (φιλέω, *phileō*, in 11:3, 36; but ἀγαπάω, *agapaō*, in 11:5); the repeated expression "the disciple whom Jesus loved" (ἀγαπάω, 13:23; 19:26; 21:7, 20; φιλέω, 20:2); people are said to love Jesus (ἀγαπάω in 8:42; 14: 15, 21, 23, 28; but φιλέω in 16:27). Note also the successive verses in Gen 37 (LXX): "Jacob loved (ἠγάπα, *ēgapa*) Joseph" (v. 3). "Now when his brothers saw that their father loved (φιλεῖ, *philei*) more than all his sons . . ." (v. 4). The same Hebrew word ('āhēb) underlies these Greek verbs.

22. As a constative aorist ἠγάπησεν (*ēgapēsen*) views God's perpetual love for humanity unitarily but accommodates specific expressions of that love within that unitary conception.

23. But there are three places where the Father's love for every obedient and loving disciple of Jesus is expressed—John 14:21; 14:23; 16:27.

24. These examples of the range of meanings of "world" are drawn (with modifications) from *The Concise Oxford Dictionary of Current English*, 6th ed., ed. J. B. Sykes (Oxford: Clarendon, 1976) 1345–46.

25. New Testament uses of the conjunction ὥστε fall into two categories.

    1. paratactic and retrospective, introducing independent

clauses and meaning "therefore," "so":

    a. with the indicative (e.g., 1 Cor 3:7)

    b. with the imperative (e.g., 1 Cor 15:58)

2. hypotactic and prospective, introducing dependent clauses:

    a. expressing an actual result and meaning "so that":

        i. with the indicative (as in classical Greek) *only John 3:16 and Gal 2:13*

        ii. with the infinitive (e.g., 1 Cor 13:2) or accusative and infinitive (e.g., 1 Cor 5:1)

    b. expressing a purpose (like ἵνα) or intended result and meaning "in order that" (according to Robertson [*Grammar* 990] there are only six probable instances—Matt 10:1; 15:33; 24:24; 27:1; Luke 4:29; 20:20).

R. H. Gundry and R. W. Howell ("The Sense and Syntax of John 3:14–17 with Special Reference to the Use of ΟΥΤΩΣ . . . ΩΣΤΕ in John 3:16," *NovT* 41 [1999] 24–39) have called into question the traditional understanding of οὕτως . . . ὥστε (*houtōs . . . hōste*) arguing that οὕτως γάρ (*gar*) is retrospective and means "for in this way" (denoting manner) (25, 39) and seeing ὥστε "as introducing a restatement of v. 14" (36) and as appropriately translated "and so" (39). But (1) it is doubtful whether *within a sentence* (as opposed to at the beginning of a sentence) ὥστε can mean "and so" and introduce an independent clause; and (2) the closely parallel Acts 14:1 καὶ (αὐτοὺς) λαλῆσαι οὕτως ὥστε πιστεῦσαι κτλ. (*kai [autous] lalēsai houtōs hōste pisteusai ktl.*) probably means "(Paul and Barnabas) spoke in such a way that . . ." (NRSV) or "they spoke so effectively that . . ." (NJB, NIV[1, 2]) rather than "they spoke in a similar way, so that . . ." The authors admit (27) that their proposals diverge from the standard lexicons and translations and they regularly reject the Loeb Classical Library [LCL] renderings of the extra-biblical references they cite.

BDF(§391[2]) prefer the reading of ὅτι over ὥστε, so that the sense would be "God showed so great a love for men (as one sees by the fact) that. . ." This reading is vastly inferior–see E. A. Abbott, *Johannine Grammar* (London: A. & C. Black, 1906) 537-38 §2697 and the comment of J. H. Moulton, *A Grammar of New Testament Greek*, vol. 1, *Prolegomena*, 3rd ed. (Edinburgh: T. & T. Clark, 1908) 209.

26. New Jerusalem Bible.

27. The alternative possible construction, with the infinitive, ὥστε ... δοῦναι (*hōste ... dounai*) ("so as to give") would have emphasized the "*connexion* between the love and the gift" (Moulton, *Grammar,* 210) between the cause and the effect, and would have elevated the cause over the effect.

28. It is not being suggested that ἔδωκεν (*edōken*) has the sense of παρέδωκεν (*paredōken*) ("gave over/up") but just as παραδίδωμι (*paradidōmi*) "is often purely synonymous with *didōmi*" (C. Spicq, *Theological Lexicon of the New Testament,* 3 vol., trans. and ed. D. Ernest [Peabody, MA: Hendrickson, 1995] 3:13) so there is a certain overlap of meaning between δίδωμι(*didōmi*) and παραδίδωμι (witness the parallelism between τοῦ δόντος ἑαυτὸν ὑπὲρ τῶν ἁμαρτιῶν ἡμῶν [Gal 1:4] and τοῦ ... παραδόντος ἑαυτὸν ὑπὲρ ἐμοῦ [Gal 2:20]) that permits ἔδωκεν to incorporate the idea of both giving and giving up (= surrendering) (cf. BDAG 242d).

29. That "giving" can involve "sending" is clear from a comparison of John 14:16 (δώσει, *dōsei*) and 14:26 (πέμψει, *pempsei*) regarding the Paraclete.

30. In this verse ἐγένετο does not mean "became" in the sense "was changed into," as when a chrysalis is changed into a butterfly and thereby ceases to be a chrysalis, but has the sense "took on" or "assumed," of the assuming of a new, additional form of existence, as when a woman becomes the mother of her firstborn.

31. See Num 21:4–9.

32. The similarities between John 3:16 and 1 John 4:9–10 are remarkable, just as the additional material in the latter passage when compared with the former is enlightening.

9 Ἐν τούτῳ ἐφανερώθη ἡ ἀγάπη τοῦ θεοῦ ἐν ὑμῖν, ὅτι τὸν υἱὸν αὐτοῦ τὸν μονογενῆ ἀπέσταλκεν ὁ θεὸς εἰς τὸν κόσμον ἵνα ζήσωμεν δι᾿ αὐτοῦ. 10 ἐν τούτῳ ἐστὶν ἡ ἀγάπη, οὐχ ὅτι ἡμεῖς ἠγαπήκαμεν τὸν θεὸν ἀλλ᾿ ὅτι αὐτὸς ἠγάπησεν ἡμᾶς καὶ ἀπέστειλεν τὸν υἱὸν αὐτοῦ ἱλασμὸν περὶ τῶν ἁμαρτιῶν ἡμῶν.

33. This view is held by (among others) G. R. Beasley-Murray (51) R. E. Brown (133, 147) D. A. Carson (206) E. Haenchen (205) A. Lincoln (154) J. R. Michaels (202–3) L. Morris (203) and R. Schnackenburg (1:399). Page numbers refer to their commentaries on John's Gospel.

34. The article with υἱόν (huion) is possessive: "his (one and only Son)". Some witnesses (p⁶³ א² A K L N T *al*) add αὐτοῦ (*autou*). The presence of αὐτοῦ in the closely parallel 1 John 4:9–10 (see n. 32 above) may have suggested the scribal addition. In the alternative attributive position of the adjective μονογενῆ (*monogenē*) "both substantive and adjective receive emphasis and the adjective is added as a sort of climax in apposition with a separate article" (Robertson, *Grammar*, 776).

35. F. Büchsel, "Μονογενής," in *TDNT*, 10 vols., ed. G. Kittel and G. Frierich, trans. G. W. Bromiley (Grand Rapids: Eerdmans, 1964–74) 4:737–38, who observes that in compound adjectives, -γενής (*-genēs*) refers to derivation or descent in general, rather than to birth in particular or to species. Etymologically, it is related to γί(γ)νεσθα (*gi[g] nesthai*) not γεννᾶσθαι (*gennasthai*).

36. As in the First Epistle of John, so in his Gospel, Jesus alone is υἱὸς θεοῦ (*huios theou*) while believers are τέκνα θεοῦ (*tekna theou*) (υἱοὶ θεοῦ [*huioi theou*] does not occur). This distinction might be expressed in a non-Johannine idiom by saying that Christ's sonship is essential, while believers' sonship is adoptive.

37. Some treat μονογενής (*monogenēs*) merely as an emphatic or fuller form of μόνος (*monos*) meaning "unique," "unparalleled," or "incomparable." Others argue for this sense on the ground that the components of the term μονογενής are μόνος ("alone," "single") and γένος (*genos*) ("kind," "species"). LSJ combines the two principal meanings of μονογενής in the definition "*the only member of a kin or kind*" (1144 s.v. μονογενής).

38. John 3:35; 5:20; 10:17.

39. When πᾶς (*pas*) is used as an adjective with an articular participle (here πᾶς ὁ πιστεύων, *pas ho pisteuōn*) it means "everyone who," or "whoever" (BDAG 782c, citing John 3:16).

40. For a discussion of the evidences for the resurrection of Jesus in the form of a debate, see Murray J. Harris, *Three Crucial Questions about Jesus* (Grand Rapids: Baker, 1994; repr. Eugene, OR: Wipf and Stock, 2008) 31–64.

41. For further details about John's distinctive use of the phrase πιστεύω εἰς (*pisteuō eis*) see Murray J. Harris, *Prepositions and Theology in the Greek New Testament* (Grand Rapids: Zondervan, 2012) 236–7.

42. See John 1:12; 4:13–14; 5:40; 6:35, 37, 44–45, 65; 7:37; 8:12; 14:5–6, 21, 23; 16:27.

43. This is not to suggest that πᾶς ὁ πιστεύων (*pas ho pisteuōn*) should be rendered "everyone who continually believes," although it is assumed that there is a continuance of faith. The articular present participle is a quasi-proper name (cf. Zerwick, *Biblical Greek,* §§371–72) that is timeless, so that this expression could be rendered "everyone who *at any time* believes." Comparable uses are ὁ ἐρχόμενος (πρὸς ἐμε) (*ho erchomenos* [*pros eme*]) "Whoever comes (to me)" (John 6:35, 37) and ὁ λαμβάνων (*ho lambanōn)* "Whoever welcomes" (John 13:20, twice). In these cases punctiliar action is presupposed in the coming and welcoming.

In the Fourth Gospel πᾶς ὁ πιστεύων (*pas ho pisteuōn*) occurs five times (3:15–16; 6:40; 11:26; 12:46); ὁ πιστεύων (*ho pisteuōn*) ten times (3:18, twice, one with a negative; 3:36; 5:24; 6:35, 47; 7:38; 11:25; 12:44; 14:12); and οἱ πιστεύοντες three times (1:12 in the dative; 6:64b, with a negative; 17:20 in the genitive). The addition of πᾶς (*pas*) reinforces the universality of the invitation or promise. The aorist οἱ πιστεύσαντες (*hoi pisteusantes*) is found only twice: in 7:39 it is a constative and timeless aorist (Robertson, *Grammar,* 859, two references) viewing believers of all time as a conceptual unit; in 20:29 it is ingressive (B. M. Fanning, *Verbal Aspect in New Testament Greek* [Oxford: Clarendon, 1990] 414), "(those who . . .) have come to believe" (NRSV). In the thirty instances of the aorist indicative or subjunctive, the aorist will have the sense "became believers" or "came to believe" or even "learned to believe;" or simply "believed."

44. So also BDAG 116a, citing John 3:16; 17:12.

45. JB; similarly TCNT, Goodspeed, ISV. In the middle voice ἀπόλλυμι (*apollumi*) means "perish," "be lost," "be destroyed." Without contextual qualification such as is found in 11:25 with κἂν ἀποθάνῃ (*kan apothanē*) ("even if he should die") it is ambiguous to translate ἀπόληται (*apolētai*) by "die" (as NEB, NAB[2]); mere physical death is not being referred to.

That the concept of "destruction" (ἀπώλεια, *apōleia*) (Matt 7:13; Phil 3:19; Heb 10:39; 2 Pet 3:7; Rev 17:8, 11) or "perishing" (ἀπόλλυσθαι, *apollusthai*) (John 3:16; 10:28; Rom 2:12; 1 Cor 1:18; 15:18; 2 Cor 2:15; 2 Pet 3:9) does not imply annihilation is clear from the use of the verb "perish" (ἀπόλλυσθαι, *apollusthai*) in John 11:50; Acts 5:37; 1 Cor 10:9–10; Jude 11.

46. In both of these verses (John 8:51; 10:28) we find the construction οὐ μή (*ou mē*) + aorist subjunctive (θεωρήσῃ [*theōrēsē*] and ἀπόλωνται [*apolōntai*], respectively) expressing an emphatic negative (cf. BDAG 646c–d) followed by εἰς τὸν αἰῶνα (*eis ton aiōna*) (literally "to eternity;" thus "for ever"). It is this potent combination that produces the sense "never ever."

47. When the ἵνα μή (*hina mē*) construction is continued with ἀλλά (*alla*), this conjunction has the meaning "but on the contrary" and ἵνα is not repeated (Robertson, *Grammar*, 1413, citing John 3:16; 6:39; 18:28; 2 John 8; and 1 Cor 12:25) but is implied (contrast οὐ . . . ἵνα . . . ἀλλ' ἵνα, *ou . . . hina . . . all' hina* in John 3:17).

48. After a negative (here μή, *mē*) ἀλλά (*alla*) introduces a contrast, not here between single words but between a negative statement (μὴ ἀπόληται, *mē apolētai*) and a positive (ἔχῃ ζωὴν αἰώνιον, *echē zōēn aiōnion*) (cf. BDAG 44c–45a).

49. For the use of ἔχω (*echō*) meaning "experience and enjoy advantages or benefits," see BDAG 421c–d.

50. These ideas would be expressed in Greek by (respectively) τὸ εἶναι (*to einai*), ψυχή (*psychē*; as in John 10:11; 13:37; 15:13), and βίος (*bios*).

51. Rom 16:26; Heb 9:14 (of the Spirit in Christ).

52. E.g., Luke 16:9 (of heavenly dwellings); 2 Cor 5:1 (of the resurrection body). For the three meanings of αἰώνιος (*aiōnios*) mentioned, see BDAG 33 c–d. In John's Gospel αἰώνιος is used only in conjunction with ζωή (*zōē*).

53. Of these 17 uses, nine are found with ἔχω (*echō*) (3:15–16, 36; 5:24, 39; 6:40, 47, 54, 68) four with εἰς (*eis*; 4:14, 36; 6:27; 12:25) two with δίδωμι (*didōmi*; 10:28; 17:2) and two in the nominative case with ἐστίν (*estin*; 12:50; 17:3).

The ultimate source of the biblical concept of "eternal life" is found in Dan 12:2 where the righteous dead are said to awake to "the life of the eternal age" or "the life of eternity" (Hebrew *hayyē ʿōlām*, in the LXX ζωὴ αἰώνιος, *zōē aiōnios*). As in John's Gospel (e.g., 5:24–25, 28–29; 6:40, 54) "eternal life" is linked with resurrection. On Dan 12:2, see Murray J. Harris, *From Grave To Glory. Resurrection in the New Testament* (Grand Rapids: Zondervan, 1990) 61–63.

If the "kingdom of God" is a central idea of the first three Gospels, "eternal life" is a dominant theme of the Fourth Gospel. The two ideas largely overlap, as is shown by passages such as Matt 19:16, 23–29 or Matt 25:34, 46. John may have avoided referring to the kingdom of God (except for recording Jesus' references to it in 3:3, 5; cf. 18:36) because of the negative political overtones attaching to the idea (cf. John 6:14–15) and because he wanted to emphasize the inward and personal and present nature of salvation.

54. Only in (John) 17:3 is ζωή (*zōē*) articular, which makes αὕτη (*hautē*) (as defined by the ἵνα [*hina*] clause) and ἡ αἰώνιος ζωή (*hē aiōnios zōē*) convertible statements (A=B, and B=A).

55. If πᾶς ὁ ζῶν (*pas ho zōn*) (John 11:26) means simply "whoever lives," the verb ζάω (*zaō*) bears a different and surprisingly weaker sense than in its immediately preceding use (ζήσεται, *zēsetai*) in v. 25. Rather, this verb has an identical sense in both verses, depicting resurrection life, both in the future (ζήσεται, "will live," v. 25b) and in the present (πᾶς ὁ ζῶν, "whoever is alive" [spiritually], v. 26a).

56. This is altogether different from immortality, if by that term we mean that the human soul is undying. Among New Testament writers it is only Paul who develops the concept of immortality. And for him it is not the survival of the soul beyond physical death, but rather freedom from decay (ἀφθαρσία, *aphtharsia*, "imperishability") and death (ἀθανασία, *athanasia*, "undyingness") that results from participation in the divine life. It is a future acquisition (1 Cor 15:53–54) not a present possession, although he did believe in the permanent existence of all humans beyond death. For "A Comparison of Immortality in the New Testament with Immortality in Plato," see Murray J. Harris, *Raised Immortal. Resurrection and Immortality in the New Testament* (Basingstoke, UK: Marshall, Morgan & Scott, 1983) 201–5.

"As for the precise relation between Johannine eternal life which has present and future aspects, and Pauline immortality which has a negative side (immunity from death) and a positive side (participation in the divine life), we may propose that eternal life is the positive aspect of immortality, and that immortality is the future aspect of eternal life" (Harris, *Raised Immortal,* 201).

57. It is significant that apart from John 17:3 αἰώνιος (*aiōnios*) always follows ζωή (*zōē*) in the Fourth Gospel.

58. One of the requirements in a doctoral seminar I used to teach on

New Testament theology was to have the students attempt to sum-marize the unifying themes of the New Testament in 120 words. Here is my own attempt:

Because God the Creator is holy and his human creatures are sinful by nature and practice, they are alienated from God. But in fulfillment of Old Testament promises God sent his holy Son into the world as Jesus of Nazareth, the Jewish Messiah, to become a vicarious sacrifice for human sin. The benefits of Christ's death and ensuing resurrec-tion are mediated by the Holy Spirit, received by repentance and faith, and enjoyed in the company of God's people in Christ the Lord's church whose mission is to proclaim and dramatize God's message of love, forgiveness, and reconciliation. After Christ's second Advent, redeemed people will enjoy bodily immortality in a renewed universe centered on Christ, but unbelievers will experience God's wrath.

59. The following points are drawn from my article, "The New Testa-ment View of Life After Death," *Themelios* 11 (1986) 47–52. Relevant New Testament passages are as follows (verses cited or referred to in the text are noted in italics). (1) *Embodied*: Luke 20:36; Rom 8:11, 23; 1 Cor 15:38, *42–44*, 50, 52–54; *2 Cor 5:1-2*; Phil 3:21. (2) *Local-ized*: Matt 19:28; Rom 8:20–22; Heb 11:16; *2 Pet 3:13*; Rev 21:1. (3) *Personal*: 1 Cor 6:14; 15:48–49; 2 Cor 5:8–10; Phil 3:20–21; 1 Thess 4:14–17. (4) *Active*: Rev 3:21; 5:10; 7:9–10, 17; *14:4*, 13; 20:6; 22:3, 5. (5) *Corporate*: Heb 12:22–23; Rev 21:1—22:5. (6) *Permanent*: Luke 20:34–36; Rom 6:8–9; 1 Cor 15:42, 53–54; 2 Cor 5:1; *Rev 22:5*.